DAILY EXPRESS AND SUNDAY EXPRESS

CARTOONS

FIFTY SEVENTH SERIES

GILES CHARACTERS™ & © 2003 Express Newspapers

Published by

Pedigree®
BOOKS

Beech Hill House, Walnut Gardens, Exeter, Devon, EX4 4DG
email: books@pedigreegroup.co.uk
Under licence from Express Newspapers
ISBN 1-904329-30-6

Gl 57

An Introduction by

Warren Mitchell

I visited with Carl Giles a couple of times, we were both sailors and yarned
sea stories till all around sloped off to bed.

Then some years ago I was honoured to unveil the statue to Giles in Ipswich.
A wonderful bronze with Vera, Gran, the kids and even the poor old family dog.
Do have a look if you're in the area.

Now leafing through this magnificent book, I'm back in those heady
post war days, a hilarious history of the times.

I hope you enjoy it all as much as me.

Warren Mitchell

"She wouldn't have played at Wimbledon in things like that when I was a girl."

"Show me a Jockey Club rule that says you CAN'T enter an automation horse in the Derby."

"I bet Charlie's cold in goal today. By the way – where is Charlie?"

"And another thing," said an M.C.C. spokesman for brighter and faster cricket,
"cut out that half-hour stroll from the pavilion to the wicket."

"We don't think you're BATMAN. We think you're a World Cup referee on the run."

"Have another look for it, boy – we've got another sixty-three matches to play today."

"No 'thanks' I don't smoke."

"Glad you've come, Harry. Gentleman left his white bubble car somewhere here while he phoned us and if we don't find it quick he's going to withdraw his annual subscription."

"RIGHT! That's the last time I meet you with your slippers and a pot of tea to cheer you up."

"Come on, Sir – admit you hate me."

"We don't have problems with 150 m.p.h. supertrains on our line, do we, Harry?"

"Dad! There's nearly six inches of it in the drive again."

"Even so, that's no way to talk to Vicar when he asked if he could expect your usual contribution to harvest festival."

"Don't go taking it out on Ronnie because the spring frost got your plants."

"Either you chuck in your job as weather forecaster or next year you go on holiday on your own."

"No, I haven't seen a missing Panda car – have you seen 250 acres of potatoes?"

"By the way – where did we leave the snow plough last year?"

"At least it's doing me garden a bit of good."

"In the first Act we come on as little Christmas fairies, and what's more we're going to try and behave like little Christmas fairies."

"Married! Well, you just get straight back in there and get unmarried."

"Seven, six, five, four, three, two . . ."

"Assuming their teachers do go on strike and we've got to have them at home a few more weeks . . ."

The Royal Commission on the Police reports that there is insufficient readiness
on the part of the public to help the Police.

"It wasn't the power cut – I just switched the light off."

"If the Americans are over here buying all our scientific talent how come they missed you?"

"We're from the Home Office to inquire if TV violence has any effect on your children. Goodbye."

"BALL BOY!"

"This Family Court charges you with unlawfully swigging Grandma's stout through a straw."

"Do you still think it was a good idea to bring him up to lobby our M.P.?"

"I think you ought to go and see what they're up to. They've been in the shed for hours with Ernie's Magic Chemistry set."

"Who shouted 'Try kicking his backside'?"

"I should keep any of them with political aspirations away from the explosives until after Guy Fawkes day."

"By the time we're a 'undred some bright client'll decide we're not too old to go back to school."

"Well, how did little Miss Bluit get on with her new class?"

"Smithy – I don't like the look of Miss Mole's auxiliary helpers one little bit."

"He made an application by phone, said he'd had several years experience, got the job."

"To detect school drug-takers, teachers have been told to look out for changes in character, standards of dress, hygiene and moods."

"And this comment from your music teacher – 'I hope your boy enjoys his holiday as much as I'm going to enjoy mine'. . ."

"On behalf of all your teachers, Ronald, I cannot express too deeply our sorrow that end of term brings us to the parting of the ways."

"He wasn't exactly shop-lifting, Madam, we caught him trying to re-plant the new school suit you bought him."

"You will all be happy to learn that because of the shortage of new teachers Mr. Chalk has volunteered to stay with us for at least another term."

"I gaze upon Chalky with wonder and I say to myself: '£40m extra on education inadequate!'"

"Introducing Super Glue for the paper chains shows a marked failure to understand the imaginative workings of the modern child's mind, Miss Winslow."

"I don't think Chalkie liked the caretaker offering him a few hours overtime cleaning the washrooms"

"We're in enough trouble photo-copying their music, without you collecting royalties under the name of Beethoven"

"Poor Penelope – she thought they were going back THIS Tuesday."

"Never seen churches doing such business on a weekday. It'll be these thanksgiving services for the children going back to school."

"Stop pushing!"

"All Bows of Burning Gold, Arrows of Desire, Spears, Swords, etc, will be placed on my desk at the front of the hall."

"This type of craft, sir, is very simple to handle – from the look of things it need be."
(Norfolk Broads)

HOLIDAY CARTOON – A quiet picnic.

Determination of the British to ensure that their sons inherit our traditional love of the sea.

"Oo said anything about peace and quiet? My advert said 'Seaside 'ut, 'arf-minute from sea, not another 'ouse for miles,' and nor there ain't."

"There'll be some hollering when we get in – I locked Grandma in the bathroom before we went away."

"Well, I *don't* think this is better than spending the week-end in Aunt Rosie's stuffy front room."

"Having a wonderful time – three days in here to get out of the rain."

"I trust I shall see something of you during the Easter Holiday?"

"This is another thing Happy Package Hols didn't include in their brochure."

"Never mind surveys proving children don't like British holidays – at 80p a go kindly look as if you do."

"You're lucky, you can have a nice easy day to get over the holiday."

"Swallowed a hundred and fourteen mince pies, three whole Christmas puddings, and seventy-six sausage rolls in one sitting."

"If you say there's nothing wrong with me every time I come to see you then you're getting paid for nothing."

"Nothing serious, Doc – large bump on your right side is only your wallet."

(Doctors got a hefty pay rise this week)

"Rodney took some pretty silly bets in the bar last night about the strength of our future policies."

"Some of us are sure keen to get on that damn council."

"Really, Nigel, you mustn't expect everybody to want the same one elected as you do!"

"Everyone else in the road have had their polling cards, Butch.
I repeat – everyone else in the road have had their
polling cards, Butch . . ."

"The last one put his coat down and bought me two gins and tonics."

"Never mind who I'm voting for – which of them let you in here?"

"Lady, don't ask me why they always have to have pictures of pretty girls to sell
their cars – just go eat your sausage roll somewhere else."

"If it's all off income tax and nothing on pensions don't be around on Budget Thursday morning, my lad."

"Mum, remember Grandma said if her pension went up she was going to treat herself to something she always wanted?"

"Incidentally, Madam, calling me a 'stuffy old pig' every time we pass in the street won't improve your chance of a loan."

"Git off, you old fool! I was only asking him the time."

"Dad – is there any rule that we have to pay Grandma Capital Gains Tax on her winnings?"

"The old fool thinks we come from outer space."

"She always was a poor loser."

"When I said she's a bit wide across the beam I didn't mean you, you old faggot."

"Me, Ducks? I'm a pop art talent scout from Balmain."

"Damn flowers – never a bottle of Scotch."

"The accused then said: 'How about a couple to take home for the wife?' Thereby commiting an act of bribery and corruption."

"I can understand Joan Collins knocking five years off, but that one stuck ten years on to get her pension early."

"Stand by for some real fireworks – Grandma's just found what's left of her hat you used on the guy."

"My boy gave the wife a nice bunch of daffs for Mother's Day."

"Day says it's Mother's Day and you're to relax and have breakfast in bed and we'll look after the house.

"It says here, Vera, that story about live alligators in the canal has been denied."

"Hang on a minute – I'm sure George would *love* to come over to tea and see the new baby. . . ."

"You'd think she was trying to tell us something!"

"I think he's nicer in the mornings since he gave up drinking."

"You stay out of this!"

"I hope not. Oh boy, I hope not."

"They wouldn't be singing their little heads off if they could read."

"Read all about it – Raise the Titanic."

"Did you see the Wildfowl Trust suggest we all 'adopt a duck' to preserve the species. Can you imagine?"

"We can have our disco here tonight – there's nothing on TV except the Cup Final"

"No problem – he'll come out in the Land Rover and tow you home – only eight miles from here, you said?"

"Now your Christmas computerised exterminator has blown the TV set, can you make it find the matches so we can mend the fuses?"

"Who set that thing to go off at 2 a.m. to remind me I've got an extra hour's sleep?"

"Women win the right to work until 65 – round here they let you work till you're 165 for free."

"We sure got sex-equality in this house – he's switched the washing machine on and lifted the ironing board from the cupboard all on his own."

(Footnote: 'Idle' men still rule the roost)

"George! Isn't it wonderful! Our new refrigerator's come at last!"

"Miss Emily, what is this I hear about a Spiv tossing you double or quits for the takings and you losing?"

"Oi! There's pixies in this 'ere park."

"Lady, don't keep telling *me* you think we're being followed by submarines – tell the captain."

"Cherry – this is Sunday. The Dairy Show finished Friday."

"The Committee feel that if you can make our candidate bear a slight resemblance to
St. George – so much the better."

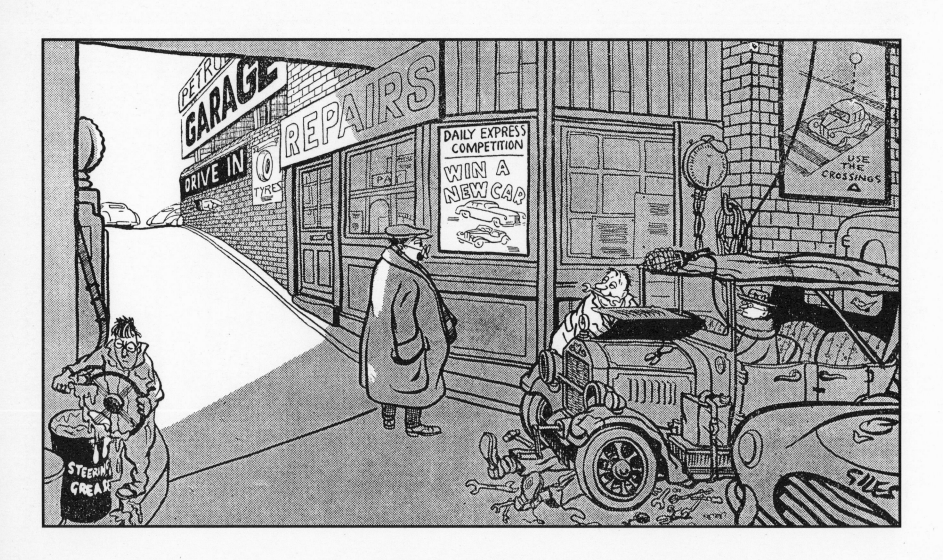

"Let's hope you don't win one, sir – we look on your old load of junk as our bread and butter."

"Rodney – have you invited a boat-load of bearded men for lunch?"

"And a Happy New Year to you too!"

"Be calm, Miss Mildred – that which fell upon your head was not radioactive fall-out."

"One little rumble from Wall Street and away go our capital gains."

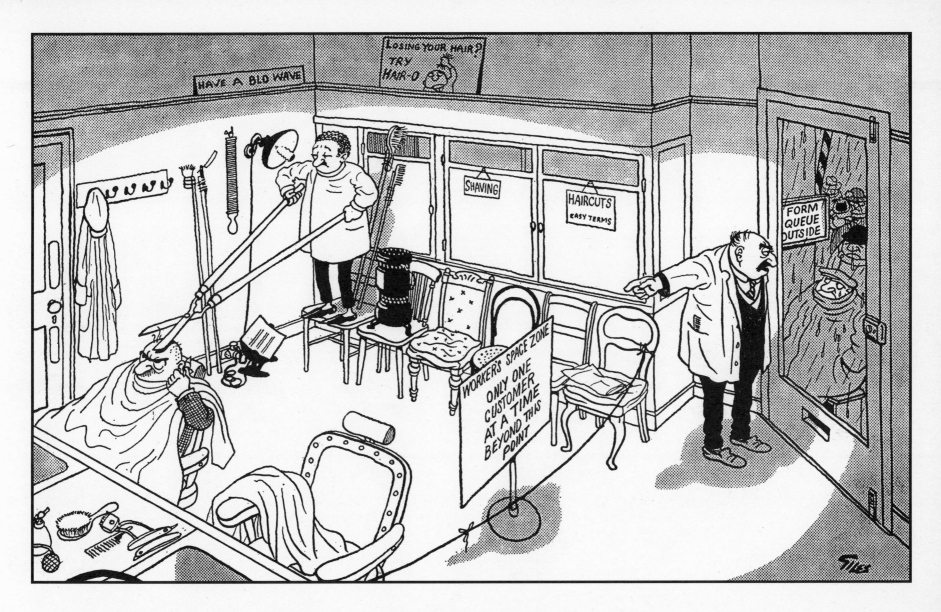

"Don't blame me, sir – blame this new law that workers must have 40 square feet of space and a minimum temperature of 60°F."

"Watch out for the niggly one with the moustache and knickerbockers –
banging away at anything that shows its head."

"Receiving picture, sir, direct from Venus."

"The blunt truth is that every marriage is different. The unexpected always keeps on happening . . ."
— Statement published by the Marriage Guidance Council.

"I distinctly told my husband to stand here and not move till I came back."

"I don't think Vicar was right to put a curse on poor Mr. Clark just because he snored through the sermon."

"Pity you dozed off, dear – you missed the bit about their aim being to provide more leisure to cushion the impact of automation."

"As a protest against Franco's demands in Gibraltar any chance of a few minutes silence on the Spanish National instrument?"

"Mr. Ramsbotham – with all due respect to your heart dancing with the daffodils and all that . . ."

"I hope this silly game isn't a stunt to divert my attentions from one of your tricks."

"I must say two in the morning of November the Fifth is a strange time to be delivering barrels of frozen herrings to the House of Commons, gentlemen."

"Compensation in this case presents certain legal problems, your erring husband possessing no less than five 'Other Women' and three 'Other Wives'."

"My Harry won't risk using the lift with possible power cuts."

"How much for one strawberry each?' I've never been so embarrassed in all my life!"

"Julie – you know your Easter bonnet –"

"Sorry to keep you waiting, M'lady – they're judging this gentleman's sheep at Smithfield this afternoon."

"His boy put it on his head at a Halloween party and he can't get it off."

"In case you're interested – it's also the Chinese Year of the Rabbit."

"Message from Supreme HQ, M'Lord – owing to increased charges by Water Privatisation M'Lady says all manoeuvres will be cut by one hour."

"Leo, this lady swears that when she came to the Zoo yesterday she had fifteen little girls . . ."

"You can relax now, Vera – they've caught the wolf and denied the escaped puma story."

"Never mind who started it – pack it up!"

"I see the Duke of Bedford's just bought six rhinos. By the way, what happened to our rhinos, Ed?"

"Come on, Charlie – let's have a little birthday smile. After all you're better off in here than they are out there."

"Yes, I saw on TV it's our last chance to save the elephant. Now get it out of the garage."

"The zoo lady said they pong a little at first, but after you get to know them, they are really quite appealing."

"When it comes to entertainment, the visitors are not exactly Tommy Coopers."

"Tell Fu Man Chu in there if he doesn't soon show, his 'Year of the Tiger' is up."

"I bet she didn't know her umbrella handle was made of ivory."

"We rescued him from the London Zoo."

MERRY CHRISTMAS

"O.K., Sister – keep moving, you're going for a ride."

"We three kings of Orient are . . ."

"You were then seen to enter yet another house where you did again wilfully distribute toys without import or export licence. . . ."

"Drunk in charge of a Zebra Crossing – that's what I am."

"Don't stand there saying 'Tch, tch, nothing's sacred.' Go and dial 999!"

"Mum! Dad's just given the carol singers a cheque for five million pounds."

"They don't sound like the words on that nice little Christmas card you sent us."

"Even if Modom was being a little difficult, telling her to go home and stuff her turkey is not keeping with the festive customer-staff relationship of our store."

"And a Happy New Year to *you* – you banal, treacly-mouthed, patronising creep."

"I don't care if Prince Charming does strangle Cinderella on TV – nobody's
going to hang the Three Wise Men and split the loot in our school play."

"Go tell Father Christmas that Mummy Christmas has come to join the office party."

"I don't think Auntie Esther meant her present to be worn OVER your topcoat, Dad."

"My Happy New Year will begin when the decorations and the last mince pie are down and not before."

"It's the Animal Liberation Front protesting about donkeys with three people up
doing Jerusalem to Bethlehem without a break."

"Last year the little dears did him up in his Christmas cave – this year he's going to be ready for them."